Springtide
RESEARCH INSTITUTE®

The State of Religion & Young People 2023
Exploring the Sacred

Our Mission

Compelled by the urgent desire to listen and attend to the lives of young people (ages 13 to 25), Springtide Research Institute is committed to understanding the distinct ways new generations experience and express community, identity, and meaning. We exist at the intersection of religious and human experience in the lives of young people. And we're here to listen.

We combine quantitative and qualitative research to reflect and amplify the lived realities of young people as they navigate shifting social, cultural, and religious landscapes. Delivering fresh data and actionable insights, we equip those who care about young people to care better.

Stay in Touch

Visit the Springtide website for a variety of resources to help you support the young people in your life, including podcast episodes, blog posts, videos, and our other reports and books. Find these resources and sign up for our monthly newsletter, *The Tide Report*, at *springtideresearch.org/subscribe.*

Connect with us at *@WeAreSpringtide* on Facebook, Instagram, or Twitter, and use *#religionandyoungpeople2023* and *#exploringthesacred* to join the conversation.

Share how you or the young people around you are experiencing Sacred Sensibility, and send us a note at *stories@springtideresearch.org.*

Contents

RESOURCES

Scan this QR code for more resources that explore the report's themes, including curated conversations with organizational leaders and young people, a gallery of photos of young people's sacred spaces, and details about our research methods.

FOREWORD

Kenji Kuramitsu

Kenji Kuramitsu is a licensed clinical social worker living in Chicago. Kenji has served as an adjunct professor at McCormick Theological Seminary and as a community-care chaplain for the Obama Foundation. In these roles and others, he has provided direct mental-health and spiritual care in medical, educational, and corporate settings. He has served on Springtide's Research Advisory Board since 2020.

"The little things? The little moments? They aren't little," notes mindfulness expert Dr. Jon Kabat-Zinn. Beginner's mind, child's pose—many wisdom traditions say that the youngest among us may be more open to *the sacred* in everyday life, being less disenchanted by routine or the strangleholds of productivity and the discomfort of uncertainty that permeate US society.

As a mental-health and spiritual-care professional, I have carried Springtide's insights with me into the clinical consulting room and into the spaces where I lead young people in learning and cultural experiences. The particular insights shared in this report have deepened my appreciation for the role of the sacred in young people's inner and outer lives. This year's annual report is essential reading for all those interested in attending to the role of the sacred in the lives of teenagers and young adults, particularly in a cultural landscape shaped by public catastrophe, private disconnection, and widespread technological access.

When asked to describe moments they consider sacred, young people tell us they encounter a mystery, an ultimacy, an interconnected awe that can increasingly give texture to the rest of their lives. Young people say these experiences are often connected to interpersonal relationships and have the ability to conjure a sense of peace and connection that is highly protective for mental health. Despite widespread skepticism toward technology, especially its ability to solve societal ills caused by capitalism and disconnection, young people still see digital space as a potential conduit for the sacred.

British psychoanalyst and pediatrician Dr. Donald Winnicott observed that for a developing young person, "it is a joy to be hidden—and a disaster not to be found." What might it mean for a young person to feel "hidden" in our technology-covered age, one where young people are expected to put their lives on display through social media? How can those who serve young people allow our mutual encounters to help us "find" and forge connections with one another as we seek to braid moments of sacred consciousness into our everyday lives?

Engaging these questions and more, Springtide has once again offered valuable sustenance to all who are helping young people navigate a safe passage on the voyages of their lives. Parents, aunts, uncles, coaches, professionals of various disciplines, and any leader who cares for young people will benefit from engaging the relevance of these findings in their own familial, clinical, campus, recreational, ministry, or academic contexts. Let us turn with openness toward the urgent and varied voices of young people, that we too may be transformed.

INTRODUCTION

The work of Springtide Research Institute exists at the intersection of spiritual and human experience. We strive to understand how young people make sense of an increasingly complex world so that those who care about them are equipped to care better. Each year we explore a different facet of young people's religious and spiritual lives.

In 2023, we turned to *the sacred*.

We surveyed more than 4,500 young people and interviewed dozens in-depth to better understand what young people *know* about the sacred; where, if anywhere, they *experience* the sacred; what those encounters are like—how they *feel* and how they *impact* the lives of young people, if at all; and, finally, how faith leaders and other trusted adults can help young people *see, appreciate,* and *respond to* the sacred in everyday life.

To do this, we first had to identify a working definition of *the sacred*. Social scientists have long debated how to define terms like *religion*, *spirituality*, *faith*, and *the sacred*. Drawing from comprehensive literature on the social-scientific study of the sacred, we chose a broad definition from researchers Kenneth Pargament and Annette Mahoney that describes the sacred as "things that people set apart from the mundane as having a spiritual character and significance."[1]

This definition allowed us to use a sociological lens to examine how young people perceive the sacred and its components, capturing expressions from various religions and worldviews. We then expanded the definition to account for the various people, places, things, and experiences young people include in their perceptions of the sacred: those things, places, or moments that feel special and set apart from others—experiences that evoke a sense of wonder, awe, gratitude, deep truth, and interconnectedness. We also asked and analyzed how young people themselves define *the sacred*.

Measuring What's "Sacred"

We measured *the sacred* as "those things, places, or moments that feel special and set apart from others— experiences that evoke a sense of wonder, awe, gratitude, deep truth, and/or interconnectedness."

Listening to young people talk about the sacred, we learned that many experiences evoke wonder, awe, and gratitude, but it was rare for an interviewee to describe a sacred moment that didn't involve a sense of connection. From a generation touted as "America's Loneliest,"[2] that young people zero in on being *connected* when it comes to the sacred feels unsurprising.

Our findings revealed that when young people experience the sacred, they experience moments that are personal, relational, and extraordinary—moments that foster interconnectedness with themselves, with others, and with something larger than themselves.

This report guides you through our findings on young people's experience of the sacred. We dive deeper into how young people define and experience the sacred and explore how the sacred impacts the overall well-being of young people. Then we look at how adults can help young people develop a Sacred Sensibility. But first, we start with a look at the broader data set to tell us about young people's religious and spiritual lives today.

Our Data Collection

Springtide surveyed a random sample of 4,546 young people between the ages of 13 and 25. Survey recruitment balanced census splits for age, gender, region, and ethnicity/race. The margin of error for the full sample is +/- 2%.

Additionally, our research team conducted 35 60-minute interviews with an opt-in sample of young people ages 13 to 25 from across the country. While the survey enabled us to collect data from a representative sample of young people about their attitudes, beliefs, and behaviors, the interviews allowed us to gather more in-depth information on the processes and meanings behind those attitudes, beliefs, and behaviors.

More details on the survey and interview instruments, as well as a description of both samples, can be found in the appendix.

RELIGION & YOUNG PEOPLE 2023

Springtide has been collecting data on young people's religious and spiritual lives since 2019. In this section of *The State of Religion & Young People 2023*, we offer the latest snapshot of the state of religion across four categories: belief, identity, community, and practice. This year's data set once again pushes back on the narrative that young people are not interested in religion and spirituality. We find that they are.

Belief

Nearly 30% of young people say they know a higher power exists and have no doubts about it, compared to 15% who say they don't believe in a higher power at all. Our surveys use the term *higher power* as opposed to *God* to account for a diversity of young people who take our surveys, some of whom do not see a higher power as anything like the God, gods, or divine sources embraced by a given faith tradition.

Which of the following statements comes closest to describing your belief in a higher power?

I know a higher power exists and I have no doubts about it.

29%

I believe in a higher power's existence more than I doubt.

36%

I doubt a higher power's existence more than I believe.

20%

I don't believe in a higher power.

15%

Two-thirds of young people say that their **belief in a higher power overrides any doubt or that they do not doubt at all.**

About one-third of young people also believe that . . .

Percentages responding "very true" to the following statements:

I see evidence of a higher power in nature and creation.

A higher power shows up in a variety of ways in my life.

I feel that God is present in both tragic and joyful experiences.

But more young people report feeling connected to the natural environment than to a higher power.

To what extent do you feel connected to the following?

● Not at all ● Slightly ● Moderately ● Highly

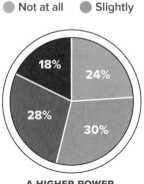

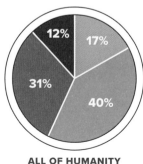

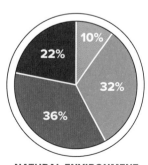

A HIGHER POWER

ALL OF HUMANITY

NATURAL ENVIRONMENT

> "I'm often searching for moments of connection to the greater universe. I find them in quiet moments where I've been writing poetry or when I'm near the ocean and in the natural world.
>
> —Emily, 19

Identity

Adolescence and young adulthood are times when young people are figuring out who they are and what they want their lives to look like in a variety of areas. Religion and spirituality are part of that mix. Many young people claim a religious affiliation with a particular faith tradition or denomination, while others claim to be nothing in particular or identify as agnostic or atheist.

What is your present religion?

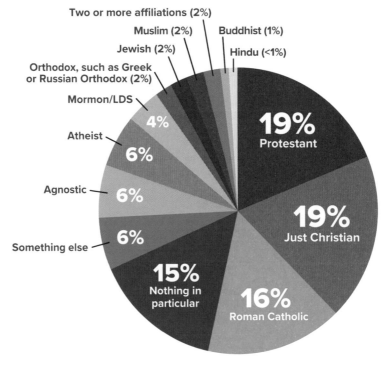

Two or more affiliations (2%)

Muslim (2%)   Buddhist (1%)

Jewish (2%)   Hindu (<1%)

Orthodox, such as Greek or Russian Orthodox (2%)

Mormon/LDS

4%

Atheist — 6%

Agnostic — 6%

Something else — 6%

15% Nothing in particular

19% Protestant

19% Just Christian

16% Roman Catholic

Percentages are approximate due to rounding.

The majority of young people say they are religious or spiritual or both. Many also report agreement with multiple religious traditions.

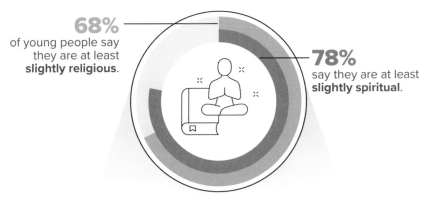

68% of young people say they are at least **slightly religious**.

78% say they are at least **slightly spiritual**.

61% of young people **identify as both—** at least slightly religious *and* at least slightly spiritual.

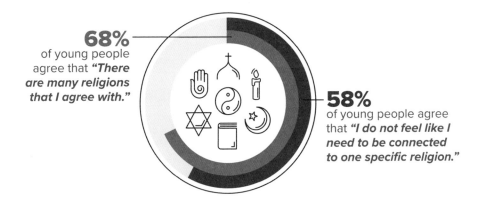

68% of young people agree that *"There are many religions that I agree with."*

58% of young people agree that *"I do not feel like I need to be connected to one specific religion."*

28% of young people say they have become **more religious or spiritual in the past few years**.

> "I'm not one of those stereotypical people who say 'I'm not religious, but I'm spiritual.' I accept all faiths and I appreciate them as is. I think every faith holds their own truths.
>
> —Melanie, 18

Young people who say they are religious

Young people who say they are spiritual

Young people who say they are **very religious** and **very spiritual**, regardless of affiliation:

10% say they are **very religious.**

17% say they are **very spiritual.**

We do not have enough Hindu respondents to make accurate comparisons, so this group is omitted from the breakdown here.

Religious & Spiritual by Affiliation

Percentages of 13-to-25-year-olds who respond "slightly," "moderately," or "very" to questions about being religious and spiritual, according to affiliation

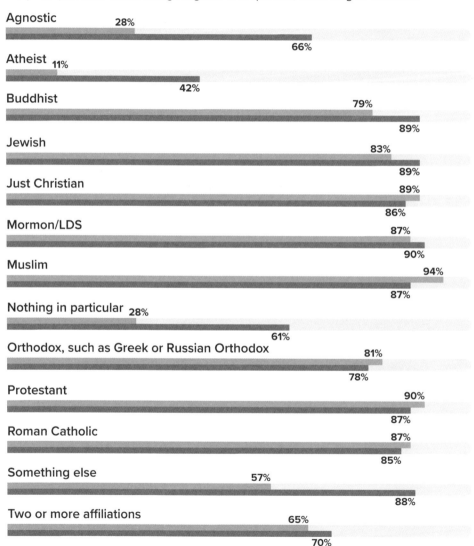

Agnostic — 28% / 66%

Atheist — 11% / 42%

Buddhist — 79% / 89%

Jewish — 83% / 89%

Just Christian — 89% / 86%

Mormon/LDS — 87% / 90%

Muslim — 94% / 87%

Nothing in particular — 28% / 61%

Orthodox, such as Greek or Russian Orthodox — 81% / 78%

Protestant — 90% / 87%

Roman Catholic — 87% / 85%

Something else — 57% / 88%

Two or more affiliations — 65% / 70%

Community

Rising levels of disaffiliation—in other words, people leaving organized religion—dominate the attention of many faith leaders concerned about religious community. Less attention, however, has gone to unaffiliation more generally. It is not uncommon for faith leaders to ask, "How do we get young people back?" But in 2023, Springtide found that 31% of young people say they've *never* participated in a religious or spiritual community. Focusing on "getting young people back" may not be helpful in thinking about how to engage them. Young people's curiosity about and commitment to spirituality and religion are increasingly taking shape in a nontraditional, nonlinear fashion and in unconventional spaces.

Which response best describes you?

● I **have never** participated in an organized religion or spiritual community.

● I **currently** participate in an organized religion or spiritual community.

● I **used to** participate in an organized religion or spiritual community.

Low or declining trust in many societal institutions, including religious ones, has been documented by Springtide studies and other social science research. In 2023, Springtide data show that almost three-fourths (72%) of young people trust organized religion only somewhat or not at all.

How much do you trust organized religion?

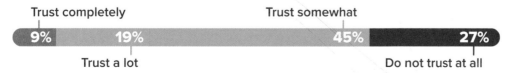

> II
>
> I listen to music [as a spiritual practice] because as the music progresses, it makes me think more about God's character and who God is. I guess to some extent it primes my heart for spending time with God.
>
> —Naima, 24

Practice

Our data show that many young people are curious about religion and spirituality and that many are committed to incorporating religious and spiritual elements into their lives. The majority of young people, however, do not attend religious services regularly.

How often do you attend religious services?

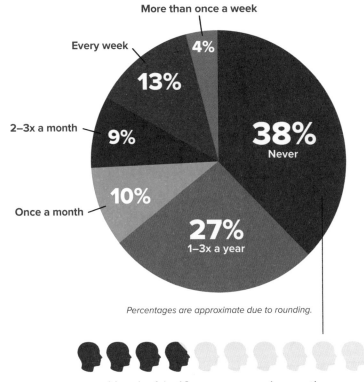

More than once a week — 4%

Every week — 13%

2–3x a month — 9%

Once a month — 10%

38% Never

27% 1–3x a year

Percentages are approximate due to rounding.

Nearly 4 in 10 young people say they **never attend religious services.**

But many young people engage in other religious or spiritual practices on a daily or weekly basis:

While you may engage in the following everyday activities, how often do you engage in these activities as religious or spiritual practices?

Percentages of young people responding "daily" or "weekly"

45%
pray

49%
read

54%
spend time
in nature

56%
engage
in art

These data provide a snapshot of young people's religious and spiritual lives in 2023. It's easy to assume that because young people report low rates of trust in organized religion or religious service attendance that they aren't interested in questions or lifestyles often associated with religion. But these data tell a more nuanced story. They also underscore the need to listen to young people on their own terms as they explore, define, and redefine traditional notions of religion, spirituality, and *the sacred*—a concept to which we turn next.

> **Many hobbies or activities have sacred elements to them. Even just conversations with your family or other day-to-day moments can be sacred. You don't have to go to a synagogue or church or mosque.**
>
> —Rhett, 22

EXPLORING THE SACRED

Measuring What's "Religious"

For Springtide, we measure *religious* as more than a reference to a particular creed, code, or system. Our methods capture and categorize a wide array of diverse impulses, questions, and connections. This approach enables us to understand meaning-making in ways that may not seem overtly "religious"—that is, formally linked to a specific tradition or institution.

In our thousands of surveys and dozens of interviews with young people, we explored many facets of *the sacred*. Specifically, we examined how young people articulate what is sacred, how common sacred experiences are for young people, what young people experience in such moments, and what characterizes these moments.

Defining *the Sacred*

In interviews, we asked young people to share with us how *they* define *the sacred*. The next page visualizes key words from their responses. The larger the circle, the more frequently the word appeared across young people's definitions of *the sacred*. 〉

Words Young People Use to Define *The Sacred*

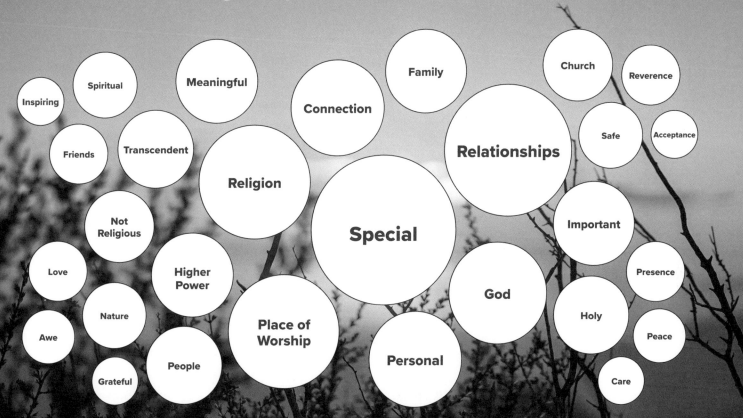

Experiencing Sacred Moments

When we asked young people if they'd ever had a sacred moment, a majority of them said yes.

Have you ever experienced a sacred moment?

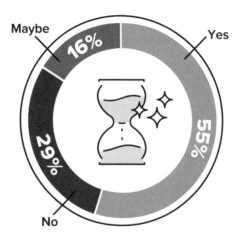

Maybe **16%**

Yes

No **29%**

55%

Sacred moments happen for young people who are Christian, Buddhist, Muslim, atheist, Jewish, nothing in particular, and more.

Percentages of young people by affiliation who say they've experienced a sacred moment

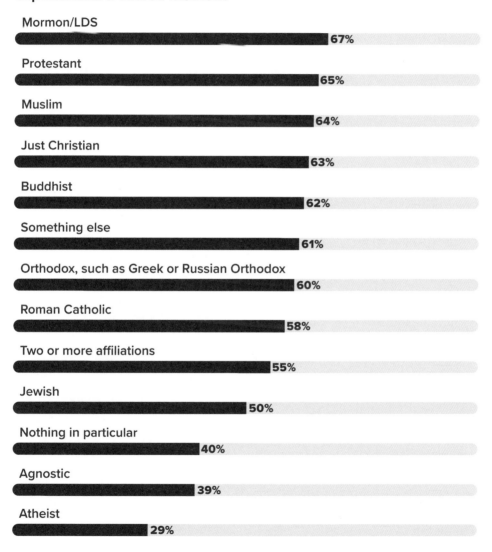

Mormon/LDS
67%

Protestant
65%

Muslim
64%

Just Christian
63%

Buddhist
62%

Something else
61%

Orthodox, such as Greek or Russian Orthodox
60%

Roman Catholic
58%

Two or more affiliations
55%

Jewish
50%

Nothing in particular
40%

Agnostic
39%

Atheist
29%

We do not have enough Hindu respondents to make accurate comparisons, so this group is omitted from the breakdown here.

The ability to "see" events and situations as sacred might be aided by having some knowledge of or exposure to religion and spirituality. When we looked at those who have experienced a sacred moment, we found that 83% also reported that religious faith is at least somewhat important in the lives of the people who raised them. Such exposure doesn't predict how young people define the sacred, nor does it guarantee they will experience sacred moments. However, exposure to religious or spiritual frameworks and language may help young people recognize something as sacred and be able to talk about it as religious or spiritual.

Sacred Spaces & Places

For Gen Z, the least religiously affiliated generation, these sacred experiences increasingly occur beyond the walls of traditional places of worship. For example, young people tell us that their encounters with the sacred happen in the privacy of their own homes more often than on hallowed grounds. Sacred moments happen with their friends on the phone and during walks on the beach. They happen when young people share their troubles with trusted adults and when they're at a concert watching their favorite band.

For example, Morrigan, 15, says the first thing that comes to mind as a sacred moment is seeing her favorite musical artist in concert:

> That was really fun to go to and connect with all the other people that love this person and love her music. It just felt like we all understood each other and like we were all one person just vibing with the music and enjoying it. I hate concerts and crowds, but I didn't even think about that—I just thought about how fun it was, and how all these people struggle a lot, but we're all connected by this artist and her music, and it all helps us . . . because her music is kind of sad. So I felt connected to all these people that I've never met before.

In which of the following have you experienced a sacred moment on more than one occasion?

Percentages reflect responses from young people who report having had a sacred moment at some point in their life. Respondents were allowed to select more than one option.

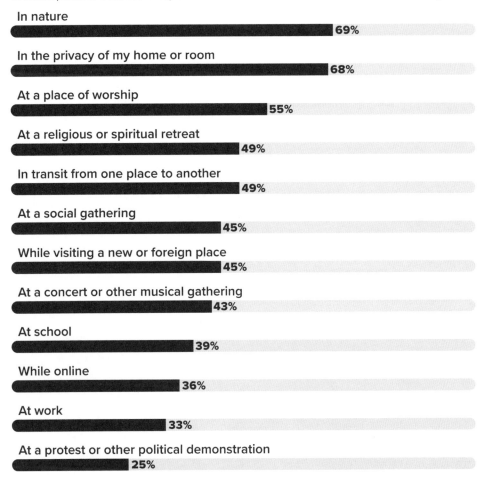

In nature
69%

In the privacy of my home or room
68%

At a place of worship
55%

At a religious or spiritual retreat
49%

In transit from one place to another
49%

At a social gathering
45%

While visiting a new or foreign place
45%

At a concert or other musical gathering
43%

At school
39%

While online
36%

At work
33%

At a protest or other political demonstration
25%

Measuring "Sacred Moments"

We measured a *sacred moment* as "an experience or encounter where you feel connected with something greater than yourself, in awe of nature and creation, grateful for your existence, or deeply connected to humanity, the universe, or a higher power."

Dimensions of Sacred Moments

It's not always the physical place that matters most. For young people who experience sacred moments, those moments aren't confined to a certain space or place. Instead, young people describe sacred moments as interrupting daily life—moments that are characterized by truth, wonder, awe, gratitude, and a sense of interconnectedness. Three main dimensions emerged in young people's definitions and descriptions of sacred moments: personal, relational, and extraordinary.

 Sacred moments are *personal*, meaning they feel tailor-made for the young person, communicating deep truths that are specific to the person experiencing them.

 Sacred moments are *relational*, meaning they are marked by profound feelings of interconnectedness.

 Sacred moments are *extraordinary*, meaning they are set apart from a young person's ordinary life in special and meaningful ways.

Sacred Moments Are Personal

At my bar mitzvah, there were like 200 people. There was my temple community, and my family came from abroad. I was already feeling happy before. And then I read a ton of the Torah portions and the Maftir, Haftarah, all of that. That was meaningful. Just seeing everyone's pleased reactions was also pretty meaningful. . . . It just felt really special.

—Noah, 19

Sacred moments often feel tailor-made for a young person, communicating deep truths that are specific to the person experiencing them. Braelin, 25, defined the term *sacred* as "something that's only for you as a person." When she was asked what things could be sacred, she responded: memories. "I guess you could say that you feel like [memories] were in a way made for you, like made for it to happen for you."

Sacred moments are shaped in large part by what is significant to the person who is experiencing them, based on their upbringing and cultural and personal identities. Emma, 21, says: "A sacred moment that I had was going to college, because not everybody gets the opportunity to go to college and not everybody graduates in four years, which I'm on track to do. So, I think getting into college was a sacred moment for me. And it also marked when I would finally get the independence that I wanted."

The personal nature of sacred moments can also reveal truths about a young person's sense of self—how they currently perceive themselves, what their aspirational sense of self is, and what they need to overcome to be the person they want to be. Melanie, 18, describes experiencing the sacred during a moment of revelation about her time in a relationship that she described as abusive: "And I just, I remember having this moment where I, where I just sat back and I was thinking to myself, 'Huh, I'm dating somebody who is definitely not good for me.' And I realized in that moment—because I have trauma of my own—if I let my trauma control me the way it's controlling him, I'm going to become like him."

What did you experience during your sacred moment?

Percentages of young people who responded "somewhat true" or "very true." Respondents were allowed to select more than one option.

I felt a sense of inspiration.
87%

I felt deep gratitude.
86%

I felt humbled.
85%

I felt intensely curious.
83%

I felt blessed.
83%

Sacred Moments Are Relational

We were up at two o'clock in the morning eating Twizzlers and watching crime shows. . . . It was one of the first times that it was just me and my mom. I felt super happy not only eating Twizzlers at 2:00 a.m. but also finally getting to spend time with my mom.

—Memphis, 15

Many young people noted sacred moments as times marked by intimate, affirming, authentic moments of connection with others. In other words, relationships become the vehicle by which young people experience a sacred moment itself. Relationships help change moments from special to sacred in several ways.

First, relationships can help young people begin to view life through a sacred lens. Elaine, 23, credits her mom for the ability to see sacred moments in her life: "My mom is one of the best people ever. She's really good at seeing everything deeper, and she always taught us to see things deeper. She always instilled in us a sense of gratitude and discernment."

Second, interactions with others help young people see themselves in relation to others, to the world around them, and to a higher power. In a world where people are connected by technology yet often still feel alone, seeing how people are linked to everything around them can be revelatory, as it was for Rhett, 22:

A few summers ago, I went backpacking out West on a hiking trip, and I had no phone, no technology at all. So just really being connected to the people around me and to nature, really detaching myself from the world, like not knowing what was happening. The intimacy that we shared together, but also just the connection to nature, was an important spiritual awakening, in a sense, and a development of my relationship with others and nature.

What did you experience during your sacred moment?

Percentages of young people who responded "somewhat true" or "very true." Respondents were allowed to select more than one option.

I felt connected to something that was really real.
87%

I felt intense feelings of loving kindness.
86%

I felt that I was in the presence of something larger than myself.
81%

I felt I was part of something infinite.
79%

I felt that I was in the presence of a higher power.
72%

Sacred Moments Are Extraordinary

I was in Greece on a study-abroad program, sitting out on the coast and watching the sunset. It was a powerful moment just to have that space.

—John, 24

Beyond sacred moments feeling personal and connected, young people defined them as moments set apart from their ordinary lives in special and meaningful ways. Erica, 21, named the sacred as "something grand" that one doesn't normally see. She also said it was "something worth protecting." Sacred moments are often characterized by the absence of interruptions—moments of quiet focus that allow young people to be fully present.

Sacred moments also are connected—and connect young people—to a deeper level of truth than is accessible in ordinary moments. Riley, 24, puts it this way: "This is important. . . . This has a deeper meaning and significance."

These moments can reveal truths to young people about who they are as individuals, what meaning exists in their lives, what their life's purpose is, and how, for some, a higher power fits into their lives. In thinking about a sermon that resonated, Miranda, 18, says: "[This sacred moment] gave me a different outlook because I've been so stressed recently, but then I realized God sees everything we do. So, I should care, but I shouldn't stress as much because God has me and my back."

The extraordinary moment can be emotional for some. Kaylee, 21, remembers wanting to cry during her sacred moment, describing it as a "whoa experience":

The emotional reaction was more like, I was just uncontrollable. It was an emotional experience in my head too . . . not that I was sobbing. I was in front of people, so I didn't want to cry, but I was like tearing up. I think I was on and off about whether there's an afterlife. Now I at least think there's something. I don't know what, but, you know, something. . . . That's been the only thing that's ever solidified that.

What did you experience during your sacred moment?

Percentages of young people who responded "somewhat true" or "very true." Respondents were allowed to select more than one option.

I felt a deep sense of peace and serenity.

87%

I felt a sense of awe.

86%

It felt unlike everyday life in a special way.

86%

I felt that existence was deeply meaningful.

85%

All distractions seemed to melt away.

82%

I felt that time had stopped.

73%

> **"**
>
> I was just lying in bed, and I started thinking about different Bible verses. . . . I started pouring my heart out to God. In that moment, I felt like my spirit laughed. I felt like God and my spirit were laughing with each other inside of my soul. My spirit was still experiencing joy amidst this grief and frustration, which in turn helped me experience joy and also wanting to heal.
>
> —Naima, 24

Sacred Moments As Multidimensional

Young people describe sacred moments happening within certain emotional states, like feeling hopeful or suffering; amid life milestones, such as graduation or the death of a loved one; and in relationships they have with those closest to them. In most cases, a sacred moment is wrapped up in all elements happening at once, combining the personal, the relational, and the extraordinary.

Notice how Erica, 21, recalls the last visit with her dying grandfather as not just personal or relational or extraordinary, but all three simultaneously:

So we were sitting there, and when I had to go, I kissed my grandfather on his cheek and told him I loved him and my grandmother . . . she was so happy because he smiled. And she was just really happy because she was like, "Look, he heard you," and it always makes me cry. It is, it was, really beautiful. . . . I was glad it made my grandmother happy because she'd spent weeks being worried about him being in the hospital, and she was obviously having a really hard time. So that really meant a lot to me.

When the young people we interviewed speak about sacred moments, they often describe internal states and external circumstances intersecting in ways that make for intensely personal moments that even when experienced alone are also relational and extraordinary. In the quote on the left, Naima, 24, shows this overlap when she recalls a time her family was dealing with her brother's mental-health crisis, and how she had a breakthrough moment during the emotional turmoil.

Despite the complex nature of sacred moments, the data show that they generally feel like personal, relational, and extraordinary experiences and that they can happen in a variety of places, spaces, and situations. Young people also experience sacred moments where all three elements are present, but whether it's one or all, these moments can have tremendous effect.

Sacred Moments & Well-Being

In our interviews with young people, we explored deeper the associations between sacred moments and well-being. We asked, "How did your sacred moment change you, if at all?" and "What, if anything, did you gain from that experience?" We learned that sacred moments make young people's lives better in three ways: by offering them direction, by imbuing their lives with meaning, and by giving them a deep sense of peace.

Young people who have experienced a sacred moment tend to report higher rates of belonging, flourishing, and life satisfaction. Young people who are at least slightly religious score higher than their nonreligious counterparts on each of the five indicators of well-being below.

Percentages of young people who have experienced a sacred moment and say they are_____ among those who . . .

● Not religious　　● At least slightly religious

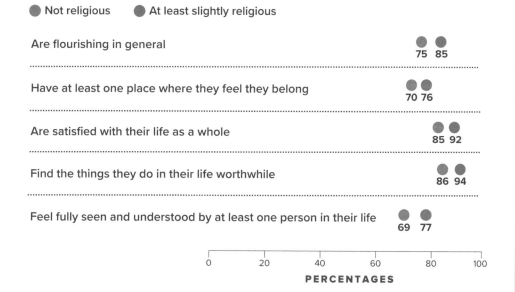

Are flourishing in general
75 85

Have at least one place where they feel they belong
70 76

Are satisfied with their life as a whole
85 92

Find the things they do in their life worthwhile
86 94

Feel fully seen and understood by at least one person in their life
69 77

| 0 | 20 | 40 | 60 | 80 | 100 |

PERCENTAGES

Young people who have experienced a sacred moment also tend to value social responsibility and demonstrate openness to disagreement and change more than young people who have not experienced sacred moments.

Percentages of young people who say they _____ among those who . . .

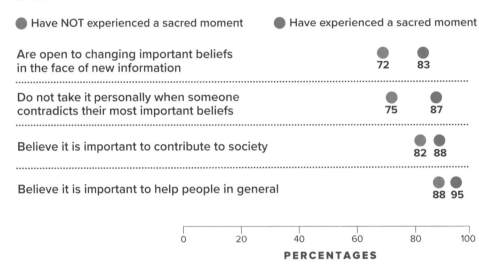

● Have NOT experienced a sacred moment   ● Have experienced a sacred moment

Are open to changing important beliefs
in the face of new information   72   83

Do not take it personally when someone
contradicts their most important beliefs   75   87

Believe it is important to contribute to society   82   88

Believe it is important to help people in general   88   95

0   20   40   60   80   100

PERCENTAGES

Social scientists have observed many ways that religion enhances well-being—for example, by elevating happiness, buffering against hardship, expanding social ties, and more. In focusing here on sacred moments, we expand an understanding of how religion matters for young people's well-being. Attending to the sacred also captures the dynamics of well-being among young people who may or may not formally affiliate with a religious tradition.

Direction

Young people tell us that sacred moments often result in what feels like positive momentum, a recognition that in that moment, something—whether it's an internal state or an external circumstance—improved greatly.

In college, Naima, 24, was part of a Black Christian organization where the Bible studies would turn into important sacred moments:

Those ended up becoming like more vulnerable moments because we were Black at a Predominately White Institution, and we were struggling in a lot of different areas. One night I was talking with one of my friends. I was telling her something really personal, and in that moment, she like met me with love and empathy. And for me, it was a beautiful depiction of, "Oh, this is how God feels about me." Up until that point, it had been a huge struggle for me to accept love from other people and from God. . . . But when we were in that space together . . . she met my vulnerability with assurance. . . . It just has made me think about this reality that redefined how I view church—removing that from this physical place and more so realizing it within the connections that we have with other folks.

85% of young people say they've **experienced intense feelings of loving kindness during sacred moments**.

Many young people also note that these experiences help them to feel better in their own skin and to be proud of the people they are becoming. Jeff, a 16-year-old transgender young man, recalls his first date with his partner, which ended in them dancing to some of their favorite songs. Jeff says he will listen to the songs if he wants to relive the moment. He explains how that experience made him feel even better about who he is:

It kind of gave me more of a sense of being more open to who I actually am rather than conforming to those around me. Rather than changing my interests up to make people feel more comfortable, I felt more comfortable being myself instead of someone else. Overall, it just made me a slightly happier and just a "more okay with myself" person.

Some young people experience sacred moments during tragic situations. Yet regardless of the circumstances around these moments, young people say the experience often helps them move from negative or neutral emotions to more positive ones. Clara, 17, supported her younger sister while she battled anorexia. Her sister's health was in such a fragile state that the time Clara was able to spend with her, minute by minute, became sacred.

People always say once you go through something tough, it makes you a lot more grateful for what you have. It also brings a lot of negative emotions, like stress . . . and responsibility and guilt, in a way. But most of it is just really positive, especially with the comparison of how things were. . . . I feel a lot of gratitude for what I have now and joy for [smaller] things.

Meaning

Regardless of the nature of a particular moment or where it stems from, most young people agree that sacred moments can be joy-inducing at least and life-changing at most. Sacred moments have the power to make life more meaningful. Morrigan, 15, shared this perspective: "Life would be less meaningful without sacred moments. They make you appreciate the good things [in life]."

Riley, 24, experiences sacred moments in the context of movie-going and reflects on the meaning of these experiences:

I joke with my friend a lot that movie theaters are like our church. I've never been to church, but I go to the movies at least once a week, which I didn't always do. . . . But going to the theater, sitting in a dark room . . . theaters are dying, so sometimes there's no one else there, but sometimes other people are there and they experience a movie with you. And I think I've gotten more involved with movies and thinking about movies and what that means for who we are and how we see ourselves. Like when I saw the movie Everything Everywhere, All At Once*. . . . I think about that movie all the time now and how it talks about how, on the one hand, you can be really nihilistic and think that we're small and insignificant and nothing matters in the world. Or you can say, yeah we're small and insignificant, but that means we get to decide what matters in the world. And things like that, that I hold onto about films I watch— especially going to see them and being really intentional about my time and space with them—I think has changed who I am and how I think about the world.*

Like Riley, Elaine, 23, says her experience of the sacred led to a change in how she thinks and who she is in relation to others:

My sacred moment connected me to a wider perspective. I'm not getting so wrapped up in my own head and in my own life [anymore]. I'm caring about other people more, and I have a more eternal perspective that [gives me] hope.

"

Having more sacred moments would radically shape how I, in general, view the world. It would be a more consistent reminder of people's worth, people's value, my worth, my value, and the impact of connections— how powerful and important they are.

—Naima, 24

Peace

Young people say sacred moments feel good and help them reflect on their lives. In interviews, they recall what some may consider a holy silence—no chatter, no devices, no notification dings and pings. As much as she didn't like going to church, Melanie, 18, recalls how going to chapel at her high school did provide a much-needed break:

> I guess all of it in the moment was just like, wow—I got to appreciate it because I wasn't looking at my phone or my laptop or anything. I got to appreciate the simple things like the glass, the statues, the seats . . . [even though] they weren't really super comfortable. But I was able to appreciate the quiet too, because you know how it is in high school. Everybody's chatting about something. So being able to be alone and just have that quietness, where I don't have to really worry about anything, it was like, wow, this is nice.

For some young people, the emotional impact of a sacred moment comes not from a specific person, place, or thing, but from a realization about one's life. For Mandy, 20, it was a random flash of recognition of how far she'd come from an unhappy homelife and difficult relationships that gave her an emotional calm:

> At that point in my life, I was [about to go] to college and finally out of my house. . . . I felt like I had a more secure friend group and relationship and everything. This one time at my old job—it was the morning, and I had gotten some tea from Starbucks—I was just driving, and I just started feeling really happy about the direction my life was going in and how lucky I was.

—————

Springtide data show that young people from all religious affiliations and those with no religious affiliation experience sacred moments. Those who have experienced such moments perceive them as personal, relational, and extraordinary. These moments—set apart from the ordinary in a meaningful way—feel tailored for the person and often affect their sense of connection to other people and/or God, the divine, or a higher power. Often young people describe all three qualities when talking about a sacred moment.

Sacred moments are more than discrete experiences that evoke fleeting emotions and reactions. Our data show that young people feel that these moments make life better. They give rise to emotions and insights, often providing young people with direction, meaning, and peace that have a lasting positive impact on their lives. Regardless of whether an adult is supporting young people in a religious or a secular space, our data encourage all those working with young people to focus on the spiritual aspect of their lives as a way to support their well-being.

Sacred Moments in Digital Spaces

In her book *Alone Together*, Sherry Turkle argues: "When technology engineers intimacy, relationships can be reduced to mere connections. And then, the easy connection becomes redefined as intimacy."[3]

In 2023, as society continues to navigate the effects of the COVID-19 pandemic, technology's impact on the way we experience the world is not as clear-cut as it once was. Digital spaces and the level of connection that happens there have grown more complex, more tangible and durable, and more meaningful out of necessity. Our research shows that interconnectedness is a key factor in sacred experiences for young people. What does that mean for online spaces, where connection may look different than in person? Here we explore the dynamics that impact sacred experiences in digital spaces.

Experiencing Sacred Moments Online

About one-fourth (26%) of young people ages 13 to 25 say they **have experienced a sacred moment more than once while online**.

There is no specific religious affiliation whose members experience sacred moments online more often than any other. Of those who say they have experienced more than one sacred moment online, 86% report some sort of religious upbringing.

Of those who say they have experienced more than one sacred moment online, 80% report that they are at least slightly religious and 87% report that they are at least slightly spiritual.

For some, live broadcasts of religious services or practices online made way for sacred moments. For example, David, 25, shares his experience watching a Good Friday service that Pope Francis led:

> *During the first year of the pandemic, I would stream liturgies online. I did feel [a sacred moment] in my living room. I'm watching TV and seeing Pope Francis doing these things live. . . . It's like my knowledge that it was live is what helped me feel more participatory in it. The Pope was addressing the believers around the world in that exact moment, in that exact place. And it's not like my house felt any more sacred than it does any other day, but I felt like I was in this sacred place—like a feeling of transportation.*

Caroline, 21, similarly sought online services during the pandemic. Reflecting on her experiences, she shares:

> *During COVID, I found different pastors from around the US, and there were definitely moments where . . . there were some things that God was showing me about how I'm thinking about things. Or where God helped me in understanding his character more.*

Yet most of the sacred moments in digital spaces that young people describe don't involve traditional services or practices. More frequently, they involve specific and strong moments of connection.

Elaine, 23, recalls connecting with a group of her friends regularly via social media and video calls during the early stages of the pandemic:

> *For a long time, literally every single spiritual moment I had was online. I was grateful to kind of be a part of that [friend group] and having those spiritual moments online, connecting with people—I mean that's mostly the core of it, just connecting with people—sharing different spiritual moments, meeting new people, just teaching and learning from other people all online.*

Memphis, 15, talks about how watching a movie over Discord (an online instant-messaging platform) with a friend gave her the opportunity for a sacred moment that she couldn't necessarily have had in person:

> *The thing that made it sacred was that it was something we both enjoyed and could have fun talking about. The reason it worked online was because of the fact that we could still get all of our thoughts out and watch [the movie] at the exact same time. We didn't have to pause it. And there weren't many arguments about what was happening because it was just me and her [talking to each other], so it was great.*

When it comes to sacred experience online, digital spaces simply act as connective tissue between the physical, the emotional, and the metaphysical. Devices, screens, and chat boxes become portals that allow young people to experience connection and the emotions that accompany it. Whether they link young people to what they perceive as the divine or to other humans, digital spaces can facilitate connection when in-person experiences may not be an option.

While many interviewees had not experienced a sacred moment while online, most believe such moments are possible. When we asked why they believe that, it boiled down to one thing: **They believe that people have the capacity to make deep, meaningful connections while online.** Braelin, 25, puts it this way:

> *I feel like if you're connecting with people over social media, you can have a sacred moment because you can be connecting with someone that in the long run can help you out a lot, mentally and personally.*

BONUS CONTENT

Watch Marte Aboagye, Springtide's Head of Community Engagement, and Rev. Anthony Weisman, a United Church of Christ minister, talk about connecting virtual spaces to in-person spiritual practices.

Obstacles to Encountering the Sacred Online

The interviewees who do not believe it's possible to experience a sacred moment while online express doubt about the human capacity to make deep, meaningful connections while online. Consider the way Erica, 21, responds to this question in the interview:

Interviewer: *So, do you think that you have ever experienced, or could ever experience, a sacred moment in an online space?*

Erica: *I don't think so. I just feel like . . . well, maybe, perhaps a little bit. But usually not like Zoom, not really, but me and my friends use Discord. So, when we can't see each other over the summer because we live so far away, we almost nightly go on Discord and talk to each other. But other than that, I don't think so.*

Interviewer: *Yeah. So, do you think that those potentially sacred moments with your friends on Discord—how do you think that compares to the sacred moments you might have with them in person?*

Erica: *I think they're probably less significant to me than the times we have in person because I feel like there isn't as much of a connection as there could be.*

Amanda, 24, has never experienced a sacred moment while online and feels like interactions over a screen are often less genuine than those in person:

So just one-on-one, person-on-person and just being in the moment . . . seeing each other's body language, everything that just encapsulates an in-person experience [it's not the same online]. With technology and all that, we can still see body language and facial expressions . . . , but I think it's a lot more genuine when it is in person just because [online] you only see like the top half of somebody, and essentially it's "fake it til you make it" almost.

> **"**
>
> Online, I feel like if that person genuinely cares about having a conversation, you can have sacred moments. The deeper the connection you have with the person or the more open and comfortable you are with that person, the more likely you are to have one of those sacred moments.
>
> —Jeff, 16

Similarly, Vijay, 17, says:

For certain religions, we can pray as a group online. But I feel kind of disconnected from the whole process if it's online as opposed to in person. In person, you feel their presence in the same location as everyone else. Even visiting the temple and stuff like that . . . it's like the physical experience you get there. You cannot replicate that online in any way.

Clara, 17, agrees and believes that physical presence is a "big component" of sacred moments:

I think in some ways it is easier to open up to people online because there's kind of like a barrier, you know? But I think that also because there is that barrier, in some ways it kind of restricts the connection. So, I think those in-person conversations and in-person connections are much more valuable to me than online ones are.

The digital space has long been one where what it means to "be real" or "have real experiences" has been redefined over and over. As technologies become more sophisticated and as we as humans become more acclimated to living simultaneously online and offline, what is truly authentic continues to evolve. Our data show that many young people believe it is possible to experience a sacred moment while online, but they feel those moments may not be as resonant or meaningful as those experienced in person.

Interest in Online Spiritual Communities

Despite this concern that sacred moments may be harder to find online, when we asked young people if they were interested in a totally online spiritual community, almost 60% were at least somewhat interested. When we asked young people if they would consider joining a totally online spiritual community, 28% said yes and an additional 25% said maybe. Of those who said they would consider joining a totally online spiritual community, 55% said they would consider purchasing a virtual reality headset/system if it were required to take part in a totally online spiritual community. The data show that while young people might have interest, they aren't sold on online spiritual communities, especially if participation requires extra elements.

Why Do Online Communities Appeal to Young People?

We asked young people who indicated that online or virtual religious or spiritual communities interest them to specify the reasons why. The majority selected "greater flexibility for my schedule" out of the six choices provided. We also found that certain reasons resonate more for specific groups of young people, including young people impacted by a physical, mental, or emotional condition as well as those who identify as LGBQ+. Check out the data breakdown on the following page to learn more.

Online/virtual religious or spiritual communities appeal to me because:

Respondents could select more than one answer.

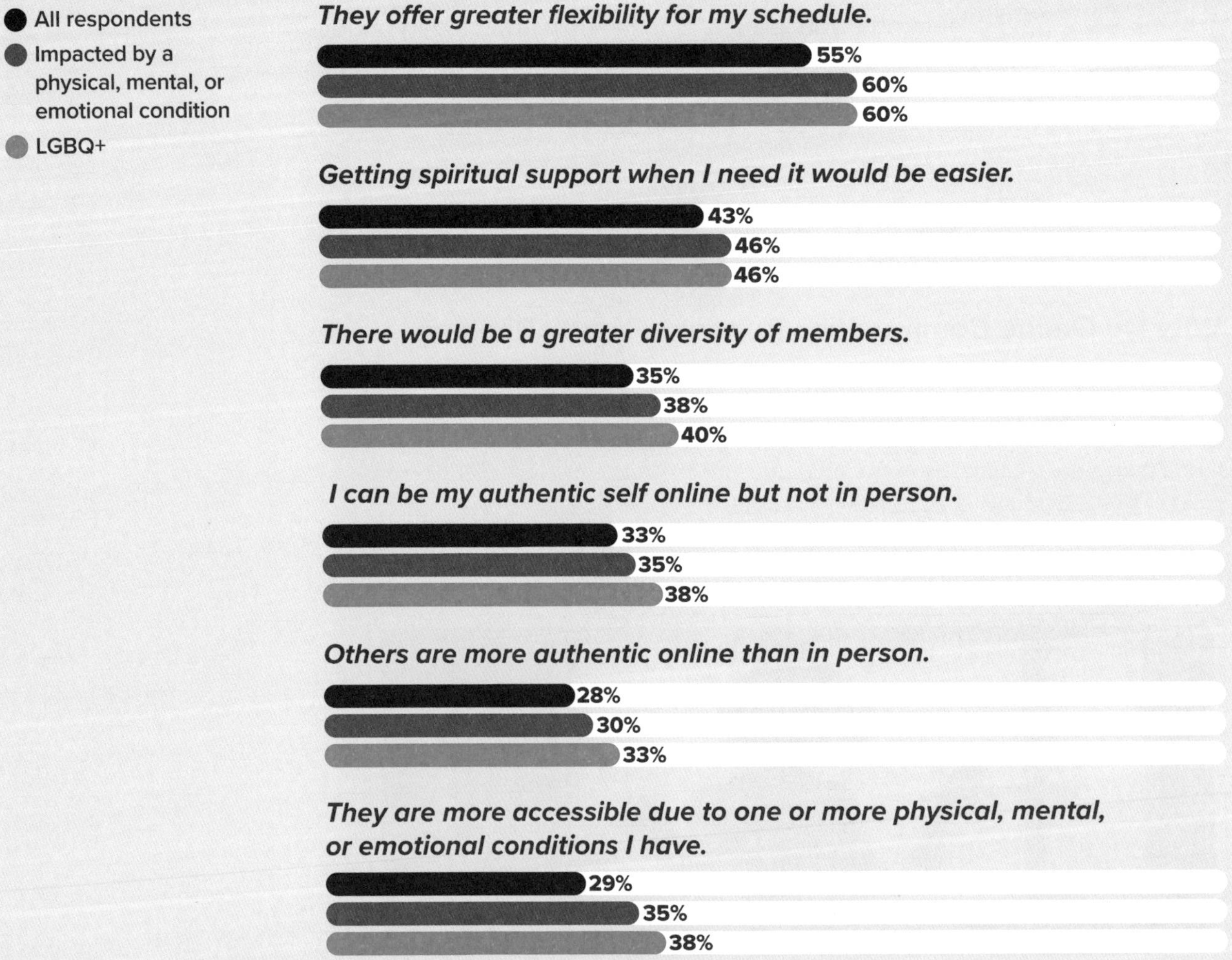

- ● All respondents
- ● Impacted by a physical, mental, or emotional condition
- ● LGBQ+

They offer greater flexibility for my schedule.

- 55%
- 60%
- 60%

Getting spiritual support when I need it would be easier.

- 43%
- 46%
- 46%

There would be a greater diversity of members.

- 35%
- 38%
- 40%

I can be my authentic self online but not in person.

- 33%
- 35%
- 38%

Others are more authentic online than in person.

- 28%
- 30%
- 33%

They are more accessible due to one or more physical, mental, or emotional conditions I have.

- 29%
- 35%
- 38%

Using online spaces for connection is still a good use of time and resources, even if not everyone experiences sacred moments online. Online spaces are not a replacement for in-person experiences, but a complement—and young people are accustomed to interacting in this hybrid manner.

Young people may not be totally sold on an online spiritual community, but that doesn't necessarily mean online spaces aren't worth experimenting with to see if they serve particular communities of young people well.

FOSTERING A SACRED SENSIBILITY

Perhaps the most important practical implication from our social scientific exploration of sacred moments is that young people have a spiritual yearning and desire to experience the sacred.

Kaylee, 21, says she'd like to have more sacred moments:

Even if they make me uncomfortable, I still want to experience them.

John, 24, says he "absolutely" would like to experience more of these moments too:

Whether they're good or bad moments or those that cause uncertainty or those that cause more consolation, I think . . . both. Bring it on. We find God in both the good and the bad moments. So, I'll take that uncertainty and all of that.

Naima, 24, speaks about knowing that her spirit seeks out these sacred moments:

That connection with the divine, that connection with God, that connection with other folks, that pure heart posture—I believe those are things that our spirit yearns for and . . . wants for us. In those moments of sacredness, my spirit theoretically wants it for me or at least wants the fruit of those sacred moments for me.

Knowing that young people desire to have (and benefit from having) sacred moments, those who serve young people may try to orchestrate sacred moments. But while the data show some common themes in young people's experiences with the sacred, the data also show that such moments cannot be orchestrated, planned, or created—even if certain conditions and personal traits are present. The data about how young people experience the sacred are not prescriptive.

In fact, very few of our interviewees mentioned a sacred moment taking place in a conventional youth group or gathering. Most of the sacred moments that young people shared with us are unplanned and spontaneous.

Mia, 23, puts it this way,

> *I think part of what makes them sacred is that they're completely unscripted, unplanned parts of life that just happen. And so, of course, I will welcome more in, but I don't wanna, like, set up for a spiritual moment, you know what I mean?*

Seeing, Appreciating, and Responding to the Sacred

Those who are looking to help young people find sacred moments won't find them in the planning, but rather in the relationship-building that forms the basis for helping young people develop what we call a Sacred Sensibility—a broader posture that enables them to do the following:

1. See something as sacred

2. Appreciate its value as such

3. Respond to the sacred with openness to exploring its meaning and significance in one's life

Helping young people approach life with a Sacred Sensibility will allow them to:

- feel connection to the divine and others in new and different ways

- find a space to reflect on and process new experiences

- better understand themselves and the world around them

- experience the emotions that contribute to overall well-being

Like compassion or humility, a Sacred Sensibility is a capacity that all human beings theoretically possess. And like other capacities, a Sacred Sensibility can be well-developed and flourishing, or it can be underdeveloped and rarely used. Trusted adults have a role in helping young people develop their own Sacred Sensibility.

To Be Human Is to Be Spiritual?

Is to be human to be spiritual? Some scientists say yes, observing that human beings have a religious or spiritual impulse regardless of context or culture. As psychologist Justin Barrett puts it, we may be "born believers" with what he terms "a god-shaped hole,"[4] while neuroscientist Andrew Newberg has documented evidence that the human brain comes hardwired to explore religious and spiritual belief.[5]

For adults working with young people, the concept of Sacred Sensibility may feel too nebulous and vague to practically apply, but Sacred Sensibility is not a program— it's a perspective. Sacred Sensibility and its elements can inform your perspective on how you approach the work you're already doing. It can inform the design of programs and retreats and also approaches to conversation and the cultivation of relationships. Knowing the elements that contribute to the development of a Sacred Sensibility can help a leader approach the work from a new vantage point.

Our data suggest the following four approaches to help young people build a Sacred Sensibility:

1. **Listen to young people.** Sacredness is personal for them. Therefore, knowing what matters and resonates with them is essential to helping them experience sacredness. While sacred moments are often unplanned, asking young people to cocreate tangible experiences can help them name and define sacredness.

2. **Don't hesitate to express your faith and beliefs to young people.** Understanding how others came into their beliefs can be helpful as young people navigate their own spiritual journeys. Be open to conversation as a way for them to explore possibilities.

3. **Help young people cultivate relationships with peers and adults in which they can be fully present and vulnerable.** This creates space for the kinds of connections at the heart of young people's experience of the sacred.

4. **Offer ways for young people to expand their horizons.** Inviting young people beyond the traditional and typical provides room for them to experience something beyond the ordinary.

In an effort to offer more in-depth practical suggestions, we turned to two practitioners and members of our Research Advisory Board to share insights that can be applied both within and outside of religious organizations. These insights offer ways to develop elements closely related to experiencing sacred moments—things like presence, attention, and connection—in order to help young people cultivate a Sacred Sensibility.

Seher Siddiqee

Seher Siddiqee is a pediatric staff chaplain at a hospital in Oakland, California. Previously, she served as the Assistant Director of Spiritual Life and Advisor for Muslim Affairs at the University of Chicago, and as Chaplain in Residence at Georgetown University. Seher has served on Springtide's Research Advisory Board since 2020.

Presence for Sacred Sensibility

Insights from Seher Siddiqee

I worked with a young adult who was hospitalized after sustaining a spinal cord injury from a gunshot wound. On first impression, he was pensive and quiet, answering questions with a few words or nods. After some weeks, a music therapist who worked with this patient told me that during her visits with him, they listened to some songs with themes of questioning God and searching for belonging. The music therapist and I decided we should visit him together and listen to songs and analyze lyrics as a way to facilitate deeper conversation about his spirituality. During our time together, we saw a shift in him, an opening to something deeper. He shared his story of growing up, taking care of his siblings, grieving losses, learning about his past, defining his family, and so much more. As I listened, I heard him share his connection with a bigger world and purpose. Music was the language of his Sacred Sensibility.

As a pediatric hospital chaplain, I encounter young people at particular moments in their journey, whether during a return visit for a chronic illness, in the midst of a new diagnosis, or after a traumatic incident. Whatever the reason for their hospitalization, it can be a moment that invites the young person to reimagine their life or reconsider who they are. For many young people, direct conversation about their identity, spirituality, or sense of belonging can be intimidating and scary, but these young people are curious about exploring these things. My experience has taught me that finding creative outlets or activities to parallel a conversation can ease some of the pressure and make it easier to build rapport and trust. What inspires me most when I talk with young people are the ways they can so easily hold the duality of pain and joy. One does not exist without the other, and it is understanding one that fosters a deeper appreciation of the other. Springtide research shows that many young people are able to recognize a sacred moment in times of joy, times of pain, or times when both are present. Sometimes the complexity of a moment is what makes it extraordinary—and therefore sacred.

I am often asked how I get young people to open up. I do not have a secret formula to share, but one key element is being a curious and nonjudgmental presence. Show up and demonstrate that you want to know them and hear their stories. Their inner thoughts and lives—as they navigate the world and figure out who they are—are just as, if not more, complex than the inner thoughts and lives of adults. I have found that many of the young people I sit with are willing to live within the spaces between categories and/or allow fluidity between them. For many, this comes from a place of curiosity and pushing back on conventional rules and teachings. Most young people won't accept statements about what is true at face value. They want to understand the layers of "Why is this important?" before they claim it as their own. At the same time, young people are willing to renegotiate their sense of self as it fits into the changing world.

Dr. Kursat Ozenc

Dr. Kursat Ozenc is a designer, educator, and author who serves as Vice President of Design at a major company. Kursat teaches classes on organizational culture at Stanford's Hasso Plattner Institute of Design and writes about work, rituals, and culture. He has coauthored two books, Rituals for Virtual Meetings *and* Rituals for Work, *that focus on helping organizations build healthy cultures. Kursat has served on Springtide's Research Advisory Board since 2022.*

Rituals for Sacred Sensibility

Insights from Kursat Ozenc

Sacred moments can be experienced in various ways, such as engaging in religious practice, connecting with people, immersing oneself in nature, or pursuing artistic and scientific interests. Ritual is one of the most powerful ways sacred moments can occur, and it's an ideal tool to create conditions for such moments to emerge.

Rituals are actions that a person or group does repeatedly, following a similar pattern or script, in which they've embedded symbolism and meaning. My team at the Ritual Design Lab (*www.ritualdesignlab.org*) has designed rituals with a wide variety of groups, and we've seen how well they can create conditions for meaningful connection. Though rituals are often tailored for a specific group, they have some universal qualities:

- Making invisible forces of life (i.e., beliefs, values) visible (and experiential) makes it easier for people to live by their values.

- Creating a space to slow down, pay attention, and recognize their surroundings helps people connect with others and feel a sense of wholeness.

- Elevating mundane moments helps people feel and get closer to things larger than themselves (i.e., community, the sacred, the divine).

Many faith traditions have time-honored rituals that can help young people feel connected to the divine and to one another. New rituals can also be designed to assist young people in developing a Sacred Sensibility. The following are four best practices that will help you design rituals for groups of young people:

1 Apply a human-centered approach.

Designing rituals means discovering the potential moments in young people's experiences that prime them for seeing the sacred. Springtide data show that sacred moments often involve an experience of positive heightened emotion. By talking to young people, you can map out their routines and identify the low and peak moments that evoke emotions. For instance, a low moment could be a long meeting for a student club. Peak moments may happen during activities where young people feel joyful and have high energy. Peak moments are insightful because they manifest what matters for your group. Once you know these moments, you can anchor your rituals around them.

2 Design rituals *with* (not *for*) young people.

When designing rituals for groups of young people, gaining buy-in will help the participants feel included. Springtide data show that for young people, sacred moments are often intensely personal. Invite young people to help craft a ritual by coming up with ideas. Encourage them to identify the values and beliefs that should be reinforced by the ritual and to select the questions to answer or activities to undertake to bring the ritual to life. Consider ritual elements, such as a metaphor that people relate to, a unique prop that serves as a symbol, or a series of bodily movements. Once the group has landed on the elements, create a flow with a beginning, a middle, and an end. Imagine that you are creating a theatrical performance: at the beginning, warm people up with a gentle introduction; in the middle, position your most impactful moments; at the end, close your ritual by winding down and reflecting.

3 Create a "meaning portfolio."

Springtide data show that young people experience sacred moments in various places and sometimes don't recognize a moment as sacred until they've had time to reflect. When designing rituals, create several and treat them as your "meaning portfolio." Use different sources of inspiration from religious practices, art, nature, and science, and treat them all as ongoing experiments. Generate a ritual "menu," and invite young people to experiment with the options until they find a few that feel right and resonate with the group. Consider linking the life cycle of a ritual to a specific group or community cycle so you can gracefully move on when the ritual loses its value.

4 Start small.

When designing rituals, start small. One strategy is to identify what's already working and look for ways to amplify it. This is called ritual spotting. For instance, several group members might already gather regularly around a specific interest. Helping them recognize such a gathering as a budding ritual can be a first step in designing a meaningful ritual and extending it to others.

Starting small also means improving existing practices. You might introduce a mini ritual to address a specific emotion or mood. For example, a daily reflection ritual could help young people express gratitude for the events of their day, or a group ritual may help participants reflect on the meaning of a shared peak experience.

Rituals elevate the mundane and offer a space with the potential to help people see the extraordinary come to life. Ritual participants experience emotions that can be transformative and gain a fuller understanding of what it means to be connected to the divine and those immediately around them. Ritual has the potential to help young people begin to see, appreciate, and respond to the sacred in their lives.

What lies at the heart of Sacred Sensibility is connection—to self, to others, and to something larger than oneself. Whether young people have had a religious upbringing or not, trusted adults can help them cultivate and develop this sensibility for themselves. As expressed through the insights shared by Seher Siddiqee and Dr. Kursat Ozenc, adults can walk alongside young people and help create literal and metaphorical spaces where they can express themselves, process what they're seeing and feeling, and create experiences where they can see the sacred for themselves. The development of a Sacred Sensibility is not guaranteed, but with time, intention, and dedicated support, young people can establish and grow their ability to see, appreciate, and respond to the sacred.

Tide-Turning Tips for Cultivating a Sacred Sensibility

The young people who participate in the Springtide Ambassadors Program (SAP) reflected on themes from this report and named activities that help them see the sacred in everyday life. They also shared specific ways other people have helped them experience the sacred. Here we offer their insights and reflections as a list of possible ways for leaders and other adults to help young people cultivate a Sacred Sensibility. *(Italics indicate quotes from SAP members.)*

All these ways and more have helped the Springtide ambassadors develop a Sacred Sensibility. Talk with young people in your life about what helps them see the sacred in their life, and reflect on whether they might benefit from new efforts in any of these areas.

 Build community.

> *I have found that being in a community of people with whom I have a close relationship opens me to seeing the sacred in my life.*

> *Being with others, whether friends or family, or even strangers, is an opportunity to see what others view as sacred. Everyone notices things differently by nature of being different people, and thus what they view as important may be mundane to me and vice versa.*

 Help young people nurture their relationships with peers and family members.

> *I see the sacred when I am with my friends.*

> *My mother has really helped me get more in tune with the spirituality and the sacredness of my life by guiding me through difficult moments.*

> *Being able to spend time alongside family is something that is necessary in order for me to see the sacredness of life.*

Help young people develop conversation skills.

Close relationships and conversations with others expand my view of what is sacred.

My brother and I, from time to time, have conversations that could be about anything from current problems in our life, the future, family, politics, etc. These conversations provide me with valuable insight that I need.

 Introduce spiritual practices.

I had a mentor during my senior year of college who taught me how to pray through The Common Book of Prayer, *and they taught me how to use guided prayer and practice meditation throughout my day.*

Every day I pray to the Hindu gods and meditate, which helps me see the sacred in everyday life.

I love spending some alone time with my Bible and soft worship music playing.

I try to spend at least 30 minutes outside with my pets, focusing on that moment and off my phone.

 Facilitate outdoor experiences.

Going to the park alone or with someone . . . shows [me] the beauty our creator blessed us with, so it makes [me] feel at peace and grateful/blessed.

When I get a view of how big the city (New York) is, it reminds me of how big the world is.

Model ways to be attentive to seeing the sacred.

I love hearing about how God is moving in the lives of those around me. This can sometimes be explicit conversations about how God is moving or just seeing the transformation take place.

When I am around a person who is kind, gentle, energetic, loving, etc., I see more of the sacred in life because of the ways they interact with others and with their surroundings.

 Express care.

Others have helped me see the sacred in everyday life by showing me values, love, time, and appreciation.

 Encourage activities specific to young people's religious traditions.

Christ-centered music, friends, family, books, and podcasts always help me see the sacred in ordinary life.

As a Muslim, praying five times a day helps me reflect and be more grateful for what I am blessed with. I can also offer praise and supplication to the Lord. Reading the Word of God helps me to gain more knowledge about life.

As a Catholic, ritual is intrinsic to maintaining the sacred as part of my everyday life. At the close of any Catholic Mass, the priest says, "Go in peace, glorifying the Lord by your life," or some variation of that, and the congregation responds, "Thanks be to God." This exchange reminds us that the sacred is not confined to four walls and one hour a week.

—

SAP participants, ranging in age from 13 to 25, represent a variety of religious and spiritual backgrounds and many regions of the United States. For more information, visit *springtideresearch.org/ambassadors*.

CONCLUSION

Young people, regardless of religious affiliation, report experiencing sacred moments. These moments, experienced both in person and online, occur in a variety of places and circumstances and give rise to such feelings as joy, wonder, awe, sadness, lament, or some combination. Whether young people realize what they've experienced in the moment or after some time has passed, these moments tend to have lasting positive effects that prompt young people to seek more of them.

Young people's descriptions of sacred moments and their impacts led us to identify a capacity we term *Sacred Sensibility*, or the ability to see, appreciate, and respond to the sacred in everyday life. Our data show that cultivating a Sacred Sensibility is directly connected to cultivating relationships with others where young people can be fully present and vulnerable. As young people develop their Sacred Sensibility, adults can help provide opportunities for interconnectedness. And as adults are present to and engage with young people, together they are able to create conditions or spaces where young people can begin to see, appreciate, and respond to the sacred in their everyday lives. Sacred Sensibility can develop over time, and trusted adults can walk alongside young people as they cultivate it.

Most of us have a desire to experience something bigger than ourselves, and some social scientists argue that human beings are hardwired for this yearning. Many young people today recognize this yearning, and they are charting their own religious and spiritual paths to satisfy it. Developing a Sacred Sensibility is a key element of this journey for young people—one that can have a lasting impact for their lives.

John M. Vitek

For 19 years, John M. Vitek served as Chief Executive Officer of Lasallian Educational and Research Initiatives, during which time he founded Springtide Research Institute®. John is the author and general editor of numerous books and articles and coauthor of Going, Going, Gone: The Dynamics of Disaffiliation in Young Catholics. *He has also served in church and educational leadership as a parish youth minister and director of religious education, a diocesan director, and diocesan chancellor.*

Thoughts on Exploring the Sacred from Springtide's Founder

Over the past four years, Springtide has been paying close attention to the ways the religious and spiritual domains of young people's lives are expressed and experienced, especially amid the profound shifts in religious institutional affiliation. Something that struck me in this year's data is that nearly one-third (31%) of young people ages 13 to 25 in the United States say they have never participated in a religious or spiritual community. For the past several years, I've been curious about what religious or spiritual identity would look like for young people who have never been exposed to the practices, beliefs, rites, rituals, narratives, and sacred texts of a religious tradition.

Despite nearly one-third of young people having never participated in a religious or spiritual community, 68% still self-identify as religious and 78% as spiritual. That is why I have been especially interested in *The State of Religion & Young People 2023: Exploring the Sacred*. I've wondered what young people, especially those who identify as agnostic, atheist, or unaffiliated—those who once were affiliated as well as those who have never been affiliated with a religious tradition—would say about how they perceive anything as "sacred" or express any sense of the sacred, either pursuing it or being pursued by it, in their lives. I am deeply intrigued to see in the data that most young people do identify experiences of the sacred in their lives.

The definition of *the sacred* varies across different world religions, as each tradition has its own unique understanding and interpretation. Within each religion, there may be variations in beliefs and practices regarding the sacred based on different sects, denominations, and cultural influences. Yet, in a society where young people are increasingly not connected to religious traditions, we still see evidence that a constitutive dimension of being human is to have a Sacred Sensibility—that is, the ability to see, appreciate, and respond to the sacred in everyday life.

The beauty of research is that it sets up future areas of exploration. Here are some of the questions I'm left with after studying this year's data sets: How will young people in the future experience the sacred, particularly if affiliation with the world's major religions continues to trend downward? How will the definitions of *the sacred* from the world's religious traditions reflect the lived experience of young people in the future, if at all? How might emerging generations who are increasingly unaffiliated with religious traditions define what *the sacred* means in their lived experience?

For many people, their moral framework and ethical principles are closely tied to their sense of the sacred, notwithstanding the fact that the relationship between the sacred and morality is complex and multifaceted, influenced by personal, cultural, religious, and philosophical factors. How current and future generations define or understand *the sacred* will have profound implications for society. This is no small matter, and it is a dimension of the human and religious experience and perceptions of young people that will be important to remain attentive to through ongoing sociological study.

APPENDIX: RESEARCH METHODOLOGY & PROMISE

Quantitative Research

For this report, Springtide surveyed a sample of 4,546 young people between the ages of 13 and 25. The data were collected in October 2022 by Alchemer, who sent invitations to a random subsample of their 2 to 3 million US respondents between the ages of 13 and 25. The sample was balanced to census splits for age, gender, region, and ethnicity/race. While our sample is nationally representative along these metrics, it is unclear how representative the sample is across metrics of religion. Survey data are therefore best understood as tracking broad patterns rather than providing precise point estimates.

The margin of error for the full sample is +/- 2%. Key demographics of this sample are indicated in the tables to the right.

Age	Valid Percent
13 to 17	38%
18 to 25	62%
Total	**100%**

Gender	Valid Percent
Girl/Woman or Transgender Girl/Woman	55%
Boy/Man or Transgender Boy/Man	39%
Nonbinary	4%
Other	2%
Total	**100%**

Race	Valid Percent
White	51%
Hispanic or Latino	22%
Black or African American	14%
Asian	5%
American Indian or Alaska Native	1%
Native Hawaiian or Pacific Islander	1%
Two or More Races	5%
Other	1%
Total	**100%**

To see the full list of our survey questions, response options, and demographics, please visit *springtideresearch.org/our-methodology* or email us at *research@springtideresearch.org*.

Qualitative Research

For the qualitative data in this report, Springtide conducted 35 in-depth interviews via telephone or video call with young people across the country who have had an experience that "evoked a sense of wonder, gratitude, deep truth, or interconnectedness" in their lives. We recruited respondents via Springtide's official social media accounts, through personal networks, and through a targeted ad campaign on Facebook and Instagram. The interviews took place between October and November 2022 and lasted about one hour each. Conversations were guided but open-ended, allowing for the emergence of unexpected themes while maintaining as much consistency across interviews as possible. A team of Springtide researchers conducted, coded, and analyzed the interviews. The table on the right presents some of the demographic data we collected from participants.

For more information on our interview sample and questions, please visit *springtideresearch.org/our-methodology* or email us at *research@springtideresearch.org*.

Funding

Springtide Research Institute® operates under the auspices of Lasallian Educational and Research Initiatives (LERI). LERI is a nonprofit, tax-exempt 501(c)(3) organization in the State of Minnesota and the sole funder of this study.

Pseudonym	Age	Race/Ethnicity	Gender
Alex	16	Hispanic or Latino	Boy/Man
Alice	24	White	Girl/Woman
Amanda	24	White	Girl/Woman
Anna	20	Asian	Girl/Woman
Aylin	22	White	Girl/Woman
Braelin	25	Black or African American	Girl/Woman
Caroline	21	Prefer not to say	Girl/Woman
Clara	17	White	Girl/Woman
David	25	Two or More Races	Boy/Man
Elaine	23	White	Girl/Woman
Emily	19	White	Girl/Woman
Emma	21	White	Girl/Woman
Erica	21	White	Gender Fluid
Gianna	22	White	Girl/Woman
Jeff	16	White	Transgender Boy/Man
John	24	White	Boy/Man
Julie	19	White	Girl/Woman
Kai	15	Two or More Races	Girl/Woman
Kairos	19	White	Boy/Man
Kaylee	21	White	Girl/Woman
Mandy	20	Two or More Races	Prefer not to say
Melanie	18	Hispanic or Latino	Girl/Woman
Memphis	15	Two or More Races	Gender Fluid
Mia	23	Two or More Races	Girl/Woman
Mick	22	Asian	Boy/Man
Miranda	18	Asian	Girl/Woman
Morrigan	15	White	Girl/Woman
Naima	24	Black or African American	Girl/Woman
Noah	19	White	Boy/Man
Quinn	16	Two or More Races	Boy/Man
Rhett	22	White	Boy/Man
Riley	24	White	Nonbinary
Sarah	18	White	Girl/Woman
Vijay	17	Asian	Boy/Man
Willow	17	White	Girl/Woman

Our Research Promise

At Springtide Research Institute, we are committed to a Data with Heart™ approach. Our approach is rooted in deep systematic listening to young people and the things they care about. It is founded on values, commitments, and beliefs that ground why we do our research, in addition to employing a variety of rigorous qualitative and quantitative methods. Our philosophy and approach are dynamic—informed by varying ways of listening to young people through our Springtide Ambassadors Program (SAP), Writer in Residence, *The Voices of Young People Podcast*, interns, and BIPOC fellows.

This series of commitments is ever-evolving, just like the diversity and context of the young people we are committed to. We commit to reassessing this philosophy in an ongoing capacity to reflect and embody our promise to be culturally informed and inclusive.

1. We are committed to listening to young people.

2. We believe that the voices of young people should shape what we study.

3. We bring our whole selves into our conversations with young people to build trust by owning our biases, being vulnerable about our own lives, and demonstrating that we are accountable for what we do and do not know.

4. We strive to deepen our understanding of young people, rather than impose our expectations on them.

5. We encourage young people to share their stories and creative expressions because we recognize that knowledge and truth are culturally bound and that young people actively shape our world.

6. We understand the value of numbers and that they are enriched by the words shared with us by young people.

7. We know that the questions are just as important as the answers and that our inquiry itself is a statement of our values.

8. We seek to break down the boxes that research often puts people into by exploring and understanding the highly variable lived experiences of young people.

9. We foster diverse ways of understanding the nuance and complexity of young people and social phenomena and are constantly expanding our methodologies to reflect what we have learned.

10. We resolve to produce knowledge that is actionable, useful, and valuable to the communities and organizations we serve.

Note: Numerals above are for reference only and not an indication of priority.

The Voices of Young People Podcast

Season 8 of *The Voices of Young People Podcast* features 12 teens and 20-somethings in dialogue with Marte Aboagye, Springtide's Head of Community Engagement, and with one another. For this season, we invited young people to share a story about an experience they would describe as sacred and to detail the ways it evoked a sense of wonder, awe, gratitude, deep truth, and/or interconnectedness.

EPISODE 1

Brandon W.
23, CA

Diana
16, CO

EPISODE 2

Brigette
23, AZ

Lensa
16, CO

EPISODE 3

Grace
23, KS

Tábatha
20, TX

EPISODE 4

Brandon C.
23, IN

Sam
17, NY

EPISODE 5

Anthony
23, CA

Claire
21, MN

EPISODE 6

Gabrielle
24, CA

Viva
21, MN

The Voices of Young People
PODCAST

Find the latest episodes on our website by scanning the QR code, or find us on Apple Podcasts, Anchor, Google Podcasts, or Spotify.

ACKNOWLEDGMENTS & ENDNOTES

Created by the publishing team of Springtide Research Institute.

Printed in the United States of America

5945

ISBN 978-1-64121-224-3

Research Team

Nabil Tueme, PhD, Principal Investigator

Jaclyn Doherty, MA, Researcher

Kari Koshiol, PhD, Researcher

Adrianna Smell, MA, Researcher

Jake Sullivan, MA, Researcher

Phylicia Thompson, MA, Researcher

Devaun Walker, MBA, MTS, Researcher

Brian Wright, MDiv, Researcher

Writing Team

Angela Patterson, PhD, Head Writer

Maura Thompson Hagarty, PhD, Developmental Editor

Kari Koshiol, PhD, Contributing Writer

Nabil Tueme, PhD, Contributing Writer

Creative Design & Production Team

Steven Mino, Creative Designer

Brooke Saron, Copy Editor & Production Coordinator

Our Thanks

We offer thanks to the Springtide Research Advisory Board, a group of practitioners and experts from wide-ranging fields. They provided guidance as we developed our research approach, and three members contributed to the writing. Special thanks to Kenji Kuramitsu for writing the foreword and to Seher Siddiqee and Dr. Kursat Ozenc for contributing reflections on helping young people cultivate a Sacred Sensibility.

Special thanks as well to the 2022 and 2023 cohorts of the Springtide Ambassadors Program. These young people, ages 13 to 25, have been regular conversation partners about young people and the exploration of the sacred, engaging in dialogue about questions and themes that arose in our research and writing. Visit *springtideresearch.org/ambassadors* for more information about Springtide's ambassadors.

Photo Credits

(All photos appear on Unsplash unless otherwise indicated.)

Page 5 Luke Porter

Page 7 Kate Darmody

Page 8 Shingi Rice

Page 8 Vince Fleming

Page 8 Vince Fleming

Page 9 Adrien Olichon

Page 9 Callum Shaw

Page 12 Ben Warren

Page 18 Ashley Batz

Page 18 Claud Richmond

Page 18 Javardh

Page 19 Dave Goudreau

Page 19 Neom

Page 20 Stephanie Krist

Page 21 OC Gonzalez

Page 22 Luisa Denu

Page 24 Clay Banks

Page 26 Alice Donovan Rouse

Page 31 Shutterstock

Page 32 Caleb Ekeroth

Page 33 Vince Fleming

Page 34 Ann Savchenko

Page 37 Adrianna Geo

Page 39 Surface

Page 42 Kyle Lugo

Page 43 Vinicius "amnx" Amano

Page 45 Luke Porter

Page 46 Brooke Cagle

Page 46 Christopher Campbell

Page 46 Match Sumaya

Page 47 Almani

Page 47 Mohamed Nohassi

Page 50 Stefan Stefancik

Page 51 Logan Weaver

Page 53 Helena Lopes

Page 56 Umit Bulut

Page 57 Daniel Mingook

Page 61 Jeffery Erhunse

Page 63 Lampos Aritonang

Page 71 Vince Fleming

Endnotes

1. K. I. Pargament and A. Mahoney, "Spirituality: The Search for the Sacred," in *Oxford Handbook of Positive Psychology* (3rd Edition), eds. C. R. Snyder, S. J. Lopez, L. M. Edwards, and S. C. Marques (2017). (Oxford: Oxford Academic, 2016), https://doi.org/10.1093/oxfordhb/9780199396511.013.51.

2. Springtide Research Institute, *Belonging: Reconnecting America's Loneliest Generation* (Bloomington, MN: Springtide Research Institute, 2020).

3. Sherry Turkle, *Alone Together: Why We Expect More from Technology and Less from Each Other* (New York: Basic Books, 2017), 16.

4. Justin L. Barrett, *Born Believers: The Science of Children's Religious Beliefs* (New York: Atria Books, 2012).

5. Andrew B. Newberg, Eugene G. d'Aquili, and Vince Rause, *Why God Won't Go Away: Brain Science and the Biology of Belief* (New York: Ballantine Books, 2002).

Learn more from Springtide's insights.

The Springtide Blog highlights insights from Springtide data in the context of discussions of current events and the lived experiences of young people.

With new updates each week, you'll discover more about young people, their mental health, religion and spirituality, and racial and ethnic identity, to better inform yourself and your work. Scan the QR codes to discover relevant insights from our most popular blog posts.

An Inside Look at Gen Z's Spiritual Practices

Gen Z and Belief: A Closer Look

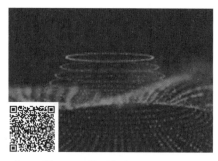

Gen Z and Religion: What the Statistics Say

More Insights on Generation Alpha

Resources for Caring for LGBTQ+ Young People

What Young BIPOC Want Faith Leaders to Know

Loneliness: 3 Ways Educators Can Support Students

How to Show Young People You Care

YOU CARE ABOUT YOUNG PEOPLE.

↓

SO DO WE.

We invite you to subscribe to *The Tide Report*, our free monthly email newsletter, for our latest blog posts that contain fresh insights and research on the inner lives of the young people you care so deeply about.

springtideresearch.org/subscribe

Bring our experts on Gen Z to your next event.

Gen Z is the most diverse generation that has ever existed, and they expect more from your organization. Springtide has the data and understanding to equip you with the insights you need to help this emerging generation flourish. Our **national speakers** each come with their own unique perspectives, areas of expertise, and skills.

Dr. Angela Patterson
Head Writer & Editor

Dr. Hannah Evans
Research Associate

Jaclyn Doherty
Research Associate

Dr. Kari Koshiol
Senior Project Manager

Marte Aboagye
Head of Community
Engagement

Dr. Nabil Tueme
Senior Research Associate

Steven Ellair
National Speaker

Dr. Tricia Bruce
Director

**Springtide Ambassadors
Program (SAP)**
Gen Z Panels

Learn more about our national speakers, and book Springtide for your next speaking engagement at *springtideresearch.org/speaking*.